Nominated for the

Poets' Prize

Mary Meriam is a rare and original poet. This is a dazzling book, a fusion of anguish and wit and song, written in clear and compelling language. I love the wildness, the inventiveness, the always surprising but accurate metaphors. She writes of real things, real people, always musically. She uses Mother Goose rhythms and rhymes or echoes of Sapphic meters or settings as grim as any of the Grimm Brothers' tales, to tell searing truths that move, frighten, and delight one with the skill of their telling.
—Naomi Replansky

Conjuring My Leafy Muse is, in numerous ways, a marvel of incantation and lyricism, a weaving of the supernatural, horrific, sensual, folkloric, and disarmingly frank. Mary Meriam's poetry has a haunting, genuine quality in which she combines the disturbing and profoundly disappointing aspects of life with a vivid, forthright nonchalance. She confesses her personal truths with unblinking sincerity. As we might infer from the title, she sometimes uses the rhythm of predetermined meter as if she were casting a spell, discovering for us and with us the exquisitely miraculous: a boiling pot of beans, a herd of deer, cottontail in clover. This is an intensely moving collection of poetry by a writer whose voice is fresh.
—Foreword Reviews

Mary Meriam is an accomplished technician and imaginative Mother Goose artist, who like Mother Goose (my favorite collection in the world), is almost always serious, even tragic, along with fun. I am floored by poems with lines like the opening of "I Learn Today My Mother Lied": *"Not one drop of Jewish blood / in me or you!" my mother cried, / as if she had a drop to hide...* We are lucky to have her dissident voice.
—Willis Barnstone

Mary Meriam is a frightening poet, a frighteningly good poet. The intensity of her writing will frighten you, but also her technical skill. She can put a chill into the most common rhyme. The poems speak like "a gust of gorgeous / thundering swallows." She identifies her models as Christina Rossetti and Charlotte Mew, whose Goblin Market and "Farmer's Bride" rightfully haunt the collection. But her real soulmate is Thomas Lovell Beddoes, the ultimate poet of the queer and scary whose masterpiece, *Death's Jest Book,* was left appropriately unfinished. She may ask us to "unspook" her dreams, but we won't succeed. The uncanny is too engrained in her sensibility. All we can ask is that she continue to keep writing.
—David Bergman

Mary Meriam is a poet who takes risks, by which I don't mean what you think I mean. There's nothing risky about breaking rules that haven't been in effect since 1880. I'm talking about the modern rules, the new respectability, the advice given in poetry workshops by legions of successful poets whom no one reads. Mary doesn't give a shit about Pound's "don'ts," she's too busy writing fierce, gorgeous poems about love and pain. She's a true rebel, in all her heartfelt, singsong, vulnerable, girly glory.
—Rose Kelleher

Mary Meriam's new collection is a treasure chest of charm and trouble. Her sonnets, lyrics and chants show the best of the New Formalism, being personal but not ever inaccessibly private, and musical without a touch of pretense. There is life and sweetness in her approach, and reproach and rue as well.
—Zachary Bos

This is my kind of a poet. 'She speaks,' as Larkin said of the beautiful and wistful and utterly different Stevie Smith, 'with the authority of sadness.' She also speaks in the language of tradition. She uses old forms fiercely. She is rather a fierce poet. Oh, and a Lesbian. You can't ignore that. But what does she do? Do with words. Magic. Above all, Mary Meriam is a magic poet and if that is what you want (as I do) this is a book for you.
—John Whitworth

Mary Meriam doesn't flinch at female eroticism, at emotional turmoil, at social upheaval, at the truth of human cruelty. She also doesn't flinch at rhyme, rhythm, formal constraint, or ancient forms of poetry and language. Even the singsong breathes fire. Mother Goose taunts the guilty mothers. But no gratuitous haranguing here: these are gut poems, deeply felt, yet adeptly and sensitively composed.
—Autostraddle

Conjuring My Leafy Muse

Conjuring My Leafy Muse

Mary Meriam

Headmistress Press

ISBN-13: 978-0615830568
ISBN-10: 0615830560

Cover Art: "Self-portrait as the Allegory of Painting (La Pittura) - Artemisia Gentileschi" (1639) by Artemisia Gentileschi - Google Cultural Institute. Licensed under Public Domain via Commons.

Cover & book design by Mary Meriam

PUBLISHER
Headmistress Press
60 Shipview Lane
Sequim, WA 98382
Telephone: 917-428-8312
Email: headmistresspress@gmail.com
Website: headmistresspress.blogspot.com

Thanks, Leafy

Contents

1. Clink the iron

The Art of Ashes

On the stones, the cinders linger,
Clink the iron, stink the stones.
Trace a pattern with my finger,
Stay away from rosy zones.

Can I make a fairy flower?
Can I draw her close to me?
Fairy, goddess, helper, mother,
Witch inside the flaming tree,

Bring your goodness to my ashes,
Bring a gold and silver gown
Bound with lace and silky sashes,
To the soot where I lie down.

In my dreams, the sound of swishes,
Like the broom that sweeps the stoop,
Fetches all my midnight wishes:
On an upswing down you swoop.

You are sweet, quick-witted, tender,
I am weepy by the wood
Blinded by the sight of splendor.
Wish I could.. I wish I could..

Plaintive Note Motel

Mother, are you lonely? I hear you sigh, then
moan in steady beats while you sleep beside me,
wounded moans, some tragedy never told me
    strangling your song-pipe.

Breath by breath, the moaning of Mother reddens,
death by drugs, flushed fugue, how she suffers sigh-sick
groans, while I, as always her daughter-stranger,
    ride my red wagons,

twist and trickle down on my twin slim bed in
Plaintive Note Motel, where we stay to witness
Kenny's wedding. Marriage, was that the trouble?
    Moaning, my mother's

stone unturned; a shot in the dark, my guesses.
Burned is Mother's everyday state, her fury
blackness brushes by on my rising nowhere,
    faster and faster.

Wolf

Mother, a wolf is wolfing me
Down. I thought I had a mother
But now I'm being wolfed. See?
Mother, a wolf is wolfing me
Down, your baby one sweet pea
Bit by hot teeth. I want another
Mother. A wolf is wolfing me
Down. I thought I had a mother.

Garden State After the War

O mommy, mommy, watermelon red,
my life is like a watermelon seed
you spit. Each night you tuck me into bed,
I need a spider swatted, or I need
the fruity sweetness of a juicy slice,
or whatsoever things are pure and true.
A bedtime story would be very nice,
your hidden past, the fact you are a Jew.
The watermelon's heavy in the bag,
and whatsoever things are good and just
are heavy too. O sweet and bitter drag,
the red, red flesh and rind of mother trust.
You are afraid, and so am I afraid.
Goodnight again, goodnight, my masquerade.

Beginning with a Line from Paradise Lost

Dreaming by night under the open sky,
waiting for heaven, I have no mother.
No, not this black-haired alien,
blood-red lipstick in the mirror.

The museum of modern art corridors,
the hallways of grade school echoing,
the stench of buses and lunchrooms,
everywhere I am, she is distant.

This is why my homework is homeless.
Only my checkered blankets love me.
Comfort me, my little pillow and bed,
dreaming by night under the open sky.

A Tragedy of Flowers

She says she is my mother, I'm her daughter.
I take a photo of her by the water,
blueberry picking, and her smile flowers.
But she abandons me in darker hours,
and so I search in the surrounding fields
for any mother-love the landscape yields.

There is a farmer with his summer yields.
I visit him as if I were his daughter
then nestle in the hollows of his fields
beside a tiny trickling stream of water,
and I weep there long and hard for hours,
twisting chains and whistles out of flowers.

There is a garden of my mother's flowers.
I wonder if the fragrances it yields
will tranquilize my mind for all the hours
I have left to be my mother's daughter;
or should I cross the muddy river water
or turn around and traipse the same old fields.

A herd of deer is bounding through the fields,
fleeing afraid, although I offered flowers.
They vanish in a hurricane of water,
and nothing in the sad sky-weeping yields
to prayers and wishes from a boggy daughter.
How much longer, harder, are the hours.

A storm's been threatening in the east for hours
and now I see it move across the fields.
It slashes lightning near the house's daughter,
my porthole's thunderstorm advances, flowers,
retreats, the way my mother never yields
a drop from all her barrels full of water.

My mother's flowers drink her howling water.
She caters to the flowers' needs for hours.
The creeper weaves, the blossom bends and yields,
and all around my mother's garden, fields
the farmer plows bow neatly to her flowers.
I wonder if she notices her daughter,

or if her daughter is a boat of water
sinking for hours or a clutch of flowers
strewing the fields until the tempest yields.

The Mother's Buttons

The mother sews with twitching round her eyes.
The daughter's wrist is bleeding in red streams.
The mother cries, and so the daughter cries.
The mother mutes the daughter's twisting screams
between her stricken breasts. The doctor stitches.
The daughter's smothered but all stitched together.
The mother knits. The mother's eyelid twitches,
and then the mother tugs the daughter's tether
tighter and tighter. And now the two at dusk
cannot forget the farmer's fragrant fields,
nor corn for dinner, shed of every husk
and boiled down. The silky twilight yields,
and goblins split the daughter's tousled head.
The daughter slides into the mother's bed.

I Learn Today My Mother Lied

"Not one drop of Jewish blood
in me or you!" my mother cried,
as if she had a drop to hide,
as if a drop becomes a flood
that drowns her in uncivil mud.
I learn today my mother lied.
"Not one drop of Jewish blood
in me or you!" my mother cried
and curtsied to the wigged M'Lud
until her Jewish spirit died.
Let my blood come back inside.
I drop her lying with a thud,
but not one drop of Jewish blood.

2. The heartbeat drums

How Beautiful She Is

She climbs the flights of palace stairs
Her gold and silver gown a charm
Whispering gone all troubles and cares
Worries and woes that cause alarm.

Tickled by rushing mountain streams
The gentle mountains kiss the sky
The sky alive with clouds and dreams
Sinking to dusk with one last sigh.

The fiddle sings, the heartbeat drums
While through the swirling, twirling court
The kindly prince of kingdom comes
As if a sailing ship to port.

Two turtledoves flush from a tree
As prince and maiden hand in hand
Begin to dance, this dance to be
A realm of peace, a fruitful land.

Scene

On the flowered couch in the dark, I see my
sister (blurred in memory) moving, sighing.
I'm a little innocent spy. A boy is
on her, excited.

Sisters doing dishes. The little sister's
weeping. Why? That boy, he was on you (taking
you so far from me). And the girl and faucet
weep in the kitchen.

Then comes clean the vase of this love for you, you
make me laugh, the night disappears, you splash your
little sister, yours, with your soft sweet flowers
flowing with solace.

Witness This

Hey little girl, come by, come by, and look.
It's time to watch your lovely sister die.
He says he wants to help, but it's a lie.
He'll steal her lovely life, by crook or hook.
He's in the kitchen, acting like a cook.
He's baking dreadful bread and poison pie.
Hey little girl, come by, come by, and look.
It's time to watch your lovely sister die.
She's sitting down. You see the bite she took?
Your tears mean nothing. Go ahead and cry.
Cry big fat baby tears and wave bye-bye.
She swallowed every morsel. How she shook!
Hey little girl, come by, come by, and look.

Orphic Chant

Let singer seek the way to hell,
and bring her back, and bring her back.
Let singer sound the hole of black,
and make her well, and make her well.
Let singer charm the deadly dell,
for knick the singer has a knack.
Let singer seek the way to hell,
and bring her back, and bring her back.
Let singer strike the silver bell.
Let singer ride the railroad track.
Let singer face the devil pack.
Let singer seek the way to hell,
and bring her back, and bring her back.

Madhouse

I'm sorry I'm too weak to break the walls.
I tried, I couldn't even shake the walls.
They call you crazy but you're only lost
sad sweet again my fingers rake the walls.
I drive to you two decades late. Forgive
my cowardice, I couldn't take the walls.
Here's where you sleep, the corner of a room.
Where is a room outside the ache the walls?
Your eyes are saying cigarettes and coffee,
the smoke the drink the pills the snake the walls.
We walk around the grounds of mental hell.
I pray for help for God earthquake the walls.
You say, *don't give the patients gifts, they'll never*
stop demanding more, they flake the walls.
A truck of groundsmen speeds by laughing leering
like you're prey for them. Mistake the walls.
I'm stupid sorry late, I'm dumb and scared,
but let me try. You must forsake the walls.
What nightmare leaves us broken as we kiss
goodbye. I'll tear them down the fake the walls.

The Stone Insanity

There's nothing I can do to change the past,
but still I am your mother, you my daughter.
I love you, and I'll show it now at last.
We sit on picnic benches near the water,
my heart in fragments on the grass. And then,
Sally's forgiven me; we're doing fine.
I know how much I hurt you two. Again,
my heart and soul slide helpless down my spine,
my hands can't catch the flowing from my eyes.
I'm sorry, please forgive me. Let me try.
To say the least, my acts have been unwise,
and all my life, I've handed you a lie.
These sweet maternal words, a wishing stream
rushing inside my mind, a mother-dream.

Rushing inside my mind, a mother-dream,
where every lie splits open, and true seeds
reach to the sun (while every dirty scheme
rots in the mulching pile with bitter weeds).
Where are my flower gifts of words for her?
I guess the world conspires to pull us low,
too many forces you could not deter,
some long-ago you never let me know.
(No pity for your daughters, heart of stone,
who tucked her babies deeply underground,
banished to stones, frozen in ice, alone,
an evil spell of exile, not one sound.)
My flowers blow away as fast as birds;
forgiveness isn't in my heart or words.

Forgiveness isn't in my heart or words,
but can I hope some supernatural hand
will send that flock of disappearing birds
back with a flower? Long enough to stand
a conversation woven in a crown?
Now listen up, my nightmare mother dear,
I'm still alive, you couldn't take me down.
Wake up, my mother-dream, my souvenir
of summer camps, piano lessons, food.
I will remember how you fed us well,
lucky for us, your rangy hungry brood,
your cats and puppies strewn around in hell.
I'm sorry for your pain, and sorry too
that there was nothing I could do for you.

That there was nothing I could do for you,
that I was nothing special in your life,
that you could simmer me for supper stew,
then calmly cut me with your fork and knife,
was swelter pain and milky wretch, was there
the house of changing hues, a ring of moods
and misery, the house of ill-repair,
each chamber with its own display of feuds,
the unraised waif discarded in a ditch,
another waif of love lost on the road,
and were you, mother, were you mother-witch?
and did you wart me like a daughter-toad,
and did you keep us parted and alone,
so that your secrets would remain unknown?

So that your secrets would remain unknown,
we lived like boarders in a troubled, hollow
silence, your phony sweetness on the phone,
the raging madness we were made to follow.
I stumbled through the fields and forests, dead
deer bones were everywhere, my tongue was torn.
Needier's land? kept pounding in my head,
and who owns this? and why I am forlorn?
I didn't understand you didn't care
if I was lost or hurt or murdered by
a beast. A child has nothing to compare.
It seemed your preference was that I should die.
As if to prove your fearsome witch's bite,
old Phillips' barn in flames inside the night.

Old Phillips' barn in flames inside the night...
We watched it from my room, as I recall,
across the fields, square in our line of sight.
It was a moonless summer night, with all
the fireflies ablaze, then Phillips' fire.
It could have just as easily been us,
but I made sure that no one would inquire,
and I would lie, and I would not discuss,
and I would hide myself forever from
the prying eyes of everyone, distract
and charm the world, until I would become
a member of society. It cracked,
this plan, directly on your daughters' heads.
Night watchmen drag us screaming from our beds.

Night watchmen drag us screaming from our beds,
while you knit sweaters in the living room
in pretty patterns, yellows, blues, and reds,
and in your garden, pretty flowers bloom.
Your ladies circle will be lunching soon,
your table is adorned with lovely plates,
a hum escapes, a merry little tune,
you sniff the hearty chowder that awaits.
Perhaps a speck of dirt is in your eye;
you never see your daughters' nightgowns flutter
in tatters down the stairs, goodbye, goodbye;
but just before we're gone, I hear you mutter,
(although the watchmen carry us so fast)
There's nothing I can do to change the past.

Out of Time

The moon, with all her starry sisters near,
moves slowly through the dark above my bed,
her clockwork ticking time off year by year,
observing both the living and the dead;
and when my tragedy of dreams is done,
all longings fully spoken for and counted,
a stronger light appears—it is the sun;
the horses of his regiment are mounted.

But once, I saw my sister in my sleep.
She held some dog-eared papers in her hand.
I wrote this novel. Take it. But the leap
of night to day will never understand
or stop for us, and she is gone again,
taking her words, her life, her book, her pen.

3. Broken bell

Cuckoo Father

Cuckoo father, hold my hand,
Come back from your cuckoo land.

Father never knew his heart,
I can't imagine how he could.
The surgeons measured every part,
And all they found was cuckoo wood.

Cuckoo father, flown away,
Come back cuckoo bird and stay.

The surgeons never made it well,
Father's heart was only sicker.
Keeping time no one could tell,
A wind-up clock, a cuckoo's ticker.

Cuckoo father, in the ground,
Come back with your heart unwound.

Sorry Show

I wish I could see him standing in the doorway of the living room.
He would have to be living. He would

have to be dancing to Big Bands on the stereo, making us
laugh because he was a grown man having a good time.

He would have to be a married man of the twentieth century,
with his mute trumpet corroding in the attic.

He kept his father's ashes on a shelf close by
his reading chair, and there an old green folder

holding my oldest poems, growing older,
and here is where nostalgia stops. Goodbye,

I could have said, my father could have said,
except goodbye requires a hello

and we were short of words.
I took his hand to cradle my heavy head,

to feel some comfort at the dinner table.
He gave me sugar-dusted toast with jam

so long ago, but was he kind? I am
his daughter from a past unstable

and burnt, with nowhere else to turn,
and for my father, of no concern.

I wish I could see her standing in the doorway of the living room.
She would have to be living. There would

have to be a doorway. Someone would have to be speaking,
or if not, listening.

World war two invades her mind again.
There is a sister left behind again.

If I could only see her one more time…
The memories begin to grind again.

Wisteria surrounds the patio
where dinner dramas will unwind again.

Which family dead steals pieces off the plate?
What solace will she ever find again?

You wretched tyrant eating like a pig—
I feel the wrench of mother bind again.

Turning me over to the muddy earth,
soaking me, and being unkind again.

I didn't know there was a war involved,
unwritten letters, love unsigned again.

The kitten eaten by the German shepherd—
be blind and deaf, and deaf and blind again.

The tissue house would have to be absorbing the hurricane
rains, and I would have to be riding my bike

up a hill so long it would have to be a mountain, or I would
have to be taking speed on the university campus.

Shot down by sorrow and weeping in the heavy brush
of scarlet-berried briers, bloodied, sounds of boots,

this the poison of the mother-witch's lexicon,
and I, a slight raw girl, stone-tongued and trod upon,

until my growing arms and legs grew into roots,
watered by my own eyes in my tortured hush.

How green the grass would have to be on the lawn around
the living room,

and how poignant the folk song
on the record player.

Why did I live? my whole life passed without you,
my helpless hands to save you, vast without you.

I've long since lost the golden chain you gave me.
The world you made for me fell fast without you.

Some say I'm not all here, or anywhere—
I can't explain the icy blast without you.

If you can hear me through the wall, don't answer—
this half a pearly shell must last without you.

Someday *la mer* may bring us back to shore.
Till then, my sorry show's miscast without you.

Why won't you love me?

Perhaps I am a broken bell,
a tumbleweed, an empty shell.
Perhaps I am a lonely child
by her loneliness beguiled,
under a witch's evil spell.

Perhaps I am an ocean swell,
a penny in a wishing well,
a piece of paper neatly filed.
Perhaps I am a broken bell,

a flower with a sour smell,
a secret locked in never tell,
a garden gone to seed and wild,
a statue toppled and reviled.
Farewell, farewell, farewell, farewell.
Perhaps I am a broken bell.

4. A hum, a hum, a hum

Crumb By Crumb

Inside the forest, I become
its sticks and twigs and silky thread
and leave my traces, crumb by crumb,

the trace of mummy, drowned in rum,
and daddy's dress in fed-up red.
Inside the forest, I become

them saying *scram,* and *do not come*
back home again to your own bed.
I leave my traces, crumb by crumb,

and ward off witches with a hum,
a hum, a hum, a hum, I said.
Inside the forest, I become

a mumbler asking, *are you dumb*
to feed the birds your tasty bread,
to leave your traces, crumb by crumb?

I wish to know where I come from,
but do not know, so walk ahead
inside the forest I become,
and leave my traces, crumb by crumb.

Lost

I ring the bell. The mademoiselle is lost?
I am, I answer, and my bell is lost.

I sell my cookies in the neighborhood,
but hopelessly, my clientele is lost.

Out on the gray-blue bouncing waves, my boat's
at sea, my fish is tossed, my shell is lost.

The menace multiplies on city streets
conquered by crows; my sad hotel is lost.

Where is my book of creatures? I could read
myself to sleep, but my gazelle is lost.

There is no love-god living on my road.
My riverbed is lost, my well is lost.

I marry no one, shadows in my eyes,
color myself, my last pastel is lost.

Animal Pity

What am I doing alone here in the park?
Caging me like a zebra in the zoo
would make me better cared for. Give me dark
to hide my horse-whipped flesh from public view.

Behind cold bars, a pair of lions screw.
In front, some jackass fools look on and mock.
A roar escapes, a roar that shakes me through.
Breaking through cage on cage, through lock on lock,

it hits Fifth Avenue, then leaps the block,
rips up the haute couture and banker's sack,
sends rippling thrills through Broadway's pigeon flock,
answers to no one, takes its grandeur back.

Now as the steel-blue evening stills the city,
I cuddle a small soft sound, a sound like pity.

The Only Home I Know

How do I know which railroad tracks to cross?
The bridge collapsed, the trail got washed away,
the highway signs went blank, the albatross
flies backwards, and I cannot find my way.
Oh world, oh world! forsythia in spring,
the cottontail in clover, leaves and snow
falling and falling over everything,
the years spin gold, go fast, go slow,
but where to go eludes me, as I drift
to bed, alone, undressed, prepared to sleep.
The crows are quiet; it's the cricket shift.
As usual, I close my eyes and weep,
my soft bed like a solitary boat
taking me somewhere, keeping me afloat.

Midnight Kitchen

You cross the river
on the bridge of your desire,
river ice, river wine, river fire
driving you to find her

practicing her cello
in her midnight kitchen,
one dim bulb yellow
in antique Pennsylvania.

You scratch the door,
your blood half wine.
She draws her bow
across your core.

No soloist, no orchestra,
has ever known
the score of silent sounds
you listen to alone.

5. Drums at dusk

Night of Snow

She lives, more lovely than sweet dreams,
Red berry lips, black hair that streams
In tender breezes through the night
Lit by starlight and pure snow white.

Meanwhile, her mother sits and schemes
Suffocating in her screams
At her own beauty's furious flight,
Old age's creeping, seeping blight.

She is the Queen, and her regime's
A bloody plot of swift extremes.
Her daughter's heart would taste just right.
She opens wide and takes a bite.

Through woods and thickets of thorny themes,
Snow stumbles through a night that teems
With lurking lowlife. Shot by fright,
She runs, and running, learns to fight.

Finally through the gloom there beams
The warm and friendly homelike gleams
Of seven gems. They are polite;
Snow's safe and snug at last? Not quite.

The lonely door has lost its seams,
Squeaks open for a witch who seems
Kindly, but murders with all her might,
To be the only belle in sight.

The tables turn again. Fate deems
The daughter live. The mother steams
In oven shoes, dancing her spite
To death, ever bitter and tight.

Sweet Woman

Did I ever know such a sweetness? Woman,
woman, when and where did I lose your scent? I
search and search my memory for those signals.
    Say I'll remember

soon, and kiss me, wake me, remind my body
lonely, touch is lovely and wanted dearly.
Woman, woman, there in the room, repairing
    close and together,

this, this thought can't conjure your hand or weight you,
ghost, blue witch, blue lack of a substance, vestige,
no, your eyes, and no, your fresh lips, and no, two
    there in the doorway.

Charlotte Mew

The she who writes of her is me.
The she who bites my lip is her.
One her, two she, and zero he.
The she who writes of her is me.
When she plus she is clearly we,
the she will show who we prefer.
The she who writes of her is me.
The she who bites my lip is her.

Sea de Sade

Marquise, dear darling bitch of decadence,
enough about your love for ancient Rome.
Let's reminisce about our close events.
You chased me, caught me, slayed me, brought me home,
proud master hunter in pursuit of prey.
Fainting I followed, wide-eyed, silent, high
on scotch and cigarettes. Quick came the day
you dumped me with a strangely sweet goodbye.
"Come here and sit," you said, "upon my lap."
"Oh, I'm too big," I moaned, "so tall, so big.
I can't." Was I so big? Well, no. Tap-tap,
you tapped, and so I sat, a sinking brig,
unmoored from the mother ship of culture, drunk
on masochism, and by a sadist sunk.

Somewhere Along the Spectrum

I take a class in feminine approach.
I hold my breath about my boyish clothes.
There is a subject I'm afraid to broach,
and for this fear I'm granted one red rose.
She smells so good, I wonder what she knows.
We leave the class together, go downtown
and dance. The beat goes fast and then it slows
until the slowness seeps inside and down.
Down to the dancing floor I fall and drown.
The dancers strip me clean of every shred
of gown and every penny in my crown.
I leave the Duchess, bleeding from the head,
naked and blind to nakedness, a mist
below the radar of the feminist.

Three Crowns of Misfortune

I. Stripper

Down the tawny, blood-red, and orange cast-offs
fall, like fairies tossing their crinkled clothing,
party-worn and faded in golden slants of
    earth-sinking sunlight;

all the Loves undone with her frock come falling,
dress undressed, unbuttoned, unzipped, Misfortune,
barefoot, rootless, stripped of her silver tree bark,
    shivers for strangers.

Not for strangers! Pitiless Love with velvet
gloves demands this stripping of leaf and costume,
downward dancing, falling forever, falling,
    falling forever.

II. Sweatshop

Wait for nothing, wait for the Loves, what matter
night that gallops, tramples her roses, horses,
wildmares, slung here fruitless and starved, Misfortune
    slips on the cliff's edge,

falls and falls with no one to catch her, over
rock face, street lamp, oceans apart from comfort,
mother, sister, lover; she sighs now, listen:
    love is unlikely.

Melancholic silkiness, cobalt, Loves hum
blue, the sidewalk saddens in Spanish Harlem
drums at dusk, at midnight, then morning traffic
    trumpets her shortfall.

III. Hack

Through the elms and ginkgos, alert to all her
listing, shrinking, deviance, sunk tomorrow,
no tomorrow ever, for sorrow's lonely
    arrows transfix her.

This is dark desertion, and silent, bitter
cold. She sits alone in the automobile,
waiting. Danger shoots her. The Loves go quickly
    somewhere without her.

Now the wheel is seized by some force outside her.
Death will drop her over the bridge. Misfortune,
desperate, poisoned, jinxed, a forgotten fire,
    fights like a soldier.

6. Shrieking creatures

The Prince of Glass

He is the prince of shards of glass,
glass bowls with Chinese stamps,
glass crystal balls with legs of brass,
and Tiffany glass lamps.

The prince has chosen to amass
glass window and glass door,
glass shelf and goblet, to surpass
his foes, who might have more.

So when he sees the lovely lass
in glass, he falls in love.
He plinks her coffin on the grass
with his glass-fingered glove.

He hates the forest's green morass
of trees and shrieking creatures;
with her in glass, they can't harass
her quintessential features.

The prince pulls out his looking glass
to check his golden locks.
The other things he does, alas,
are unseen from her box.

Obodowka Cemetery

This is dark, this time hell-sent,
This fending off the pack
That for your body tussles, bent
To sniff you and attack.

Already dogs have snapped away
Both your sister's feet.
Your naked little son is prey
They tore apart to eat.

Your body lies in sparkling frost
So new you seem to move.
My hands can only scrape a lost
Grave, a shallow groove!

Tomorrow, you and they must rot
Together in one pit.
I'd gladly go with you, and not
Wander off from it.

(after Alfred Kittner's "Friedhof Obodowka")

Arondeus

Is this why I was born,
to dress in rags and beg from friends?
Put here to paint, to write?

I met a man who labors to feed us,
barely fed. My Jan, remember
how naked moonlight filled our bed?

When the blackest dogs
broke loose, I heard an angel
tell me how to move,

to bomb our registry of papers,
blast our names and numbers;
the Nazis' fangs dissolved in vapors.

My last words before they shot me:
Laat het bekend worden dat homoseksuelen geen lafaards zijn!
Let it be known that homosexuals are not cowards!

Dinner

Tonight I set the dinner table for
the remnants of my phantom family.
Here is the marriage spent in fantasy,
here is my stillborn brother, here is war
that wiped out all my relatives and tore
my mother's mind to pieces, here is me,
here is a place beside me for big tree,
and here's my sister shot down with a roar.
We flipped and landed upside down in hell,
no parachutes, just higher, hotter flames
burning our places right down to our names.
The empty plates have nothing left to tell.
Here is a table, here a fork and knife,
here is the phantom of a better life.

Pine Needles on Snow

Let me go, my memories, sack my country,
set a fire to it, release my dying,
let my natal mind be at peace. I'm ready.
    Lose me forever.

Couldn't, didn't, wanted to save my village,
crawled the corridors underground, kept hoping
this was it. I thought this was earth, my planet,
    people who loved me.

Saving, raving mad, they are all collapsing
buildings, crouched on streets, unforgiving, desperate,
crazy. Let the savior defeat the witness,
    finish the story.

7. Burn and hum

Baptist Faggot Dinosaur

I'm at pump ten trying to sound rational in my mind. What is this gas, dinosaur bones? Then a siren, and since this is Arkansas, I hear a cop screaming faggots. Yes, I think gas comes from Earth, and that's where dinosaur bones are piled. They had to die somewhere, right? There must be tons of bones and dinosaur teeth. A van of baptists from Oklahoma stops at pump nine. They're from Earth too. I think Earth is made of dinosaurs, which were almost as big as Earth. One foot was like as big as Hawaii. They hopped around from Hawaii to Alaska to Manhattan. Continental drifts and divides meant nothing to them.

I'll Call Him Art

Art is undone. His chair's askew. His eyes,
his eyes are locked with mine. His look is raw,
mascara running, caught by small-town law,
the bible belt, bewildered parents' sighs.

Art is a man-child boy-girl compromise,
sitting between his farmer maw and paw,
here in the sheriff's office, Satan's claw.
Art holds the Word of God, holds back his cries.

I'm helpless, Art, to save you, where we are.
I try to say all this with one quick glance
before I go. Let's both go, shed the scar
of twisted stares. Let's cut and run. Let's dance.
You'll tell me all about it in the car.
Coyote-howl away the circumstance.

The Ozarks in 2004

On days like this, when no one knows or cares,
I'm sitting with her in connected chairs
that roll the thigh to touch the other's thigh,
this minor touch a dreamy contact high.
While most of me is focused on our mission,
I do consider this a good position.

She stands in front of me against a wall,
we stand together in a narrow hall,
perhaps she's climbing in her mountain mind.
I shift from foot to foot, and when I find
my voice, we talk a while about back East.
She's homesick. So am I, to say the least.

Police with guns stand guard against the crowd
gathered to hear her speech. I sit there proud
and frightened while her words burn and hum,
securing for us the auditorium.
She gives us courage, and we give her cheers,
but still this hateful place can kill us queers.

The Sum of Fall

Outside, surprised, you see a flare of red.
It is a fox, lit by the sun, I said.
The fox glides by. That is the sum of fall
for us, outdoors. Then you give Steve a call
about the trees to trim and dead tree wood
that he should cart away. *Is Thursday good?*

As good as fox can get, whose gliding's good,
whose tail in slanted sun turns fire-red.
*Please take the fifty-foot dead ash, for wood
to sell or burn as you see fit,* you said
to Steve. He'd check his week then give a call.
The red fox-tail, the walk we took this fall.

The ash is dead, and wind could make it fall
right on our house, with us inside. Not good
how long it took to give this guy a call.
I try to hold the image tight, fox-red
in slanted sun, the glide. Steve called and said
that Thursday still is looking good; he would

be here to chop the ash tree down for firewood.
I stand outside with Steve. *The ash will fall
safely, away from us, I'm safe,* he said,
this giant fireman. I see he's good
with ladders, ropes, and saws. He's used to red-
hot crises, used to falls, the desperate call,

but does Steve know we had no one to call
when they would burn our house like firewood?
They torched bonfires day and night, the red
flame flicking near our house, in spring and fall,
the devils tried to drive us out for good.
You don't belong with us, the sheriff said.

Get out, get lost, go back, the whole world said.
We stay inside; there's no one left to call
but Steve, who felled the dead tree, clean and good,
then sawed the trunk in chunks and took the wood
to sell or burn, as he sees fit. The fall
leaves turn, lit by the sun, turn gold and red,

but we were good, no matter what they said.
The wild geese call, we saw the red fox glide,
and creatures cry all through the wood in fall.

Done

Quarter to nine, the trouble in the sink is done.
The trouble from a day spent on the brink is done.

The walk we took at two, the two of us alone
in weather strangely warmer, in a blink is done.

The field of small white asters, bees and butterflies,
the buzz and scent of them, the pleasant stink is done.

It happens every fall, the leaves are green then gone,
scattered and run aground, poor leaf, its link is done.

Even with so much earthly danger, even so,
we're never done with love, or what we think is done.

I've felt her soothing over me, the sweetest spirit.
She is ineffable, so Mary's ink is done.

8. Thundering swallows

Conjuring My Leafy Muse

Dear lady of the lake,
don't leave me stranded here
with owls and mousey prey.
You take my ache away.
I need your hands to hold me,
not to tease.
I park my rusty car on leaves,
all layered, wet, and brown,
and see the sky, all pewter gray.
Down the slope,
the lake is higher,
not so far from where I stand.
I just can't read your eyes
that shine like spring Nebraska skies,
your pale Midwestern prairie eyes
that show no depth
and give no clues.
The earth accepts the sun.
The earth accepts the moon.
We live our days and nights
on earth apart.

Dear pot of boiling beans,
you boil over.
You dance away.
You care for nothing but the dance.
You sound a little sad.
Retracing steps I knew,
a narrow hall,
the dressing room,
I knock.
I knew the sea inspired you while you swam.
I felt the buzz you felt in Provincetown.
I miss the scene,
secluded like a nun.
You know the tricks of distance,
the games that words can play.
I'm in the sticks, with beans.
I like how you've got better things to do.
You're grounded.
I wonder if I sounded
contrite, controlled, confused,
or simply gone.

Dear treasure chest of trouble,
crows fly around my house.
The mob is after me, they mock and sneer.
Deep inside my quiet room, I hear
your heart beat slow.
Your hair is loose and shines like gems.
I sail away and live on waves of you,
my pale disheveled body
finding harbor here,
my love, my dear.
I pluck a rose with petals
soft and swollen, scented sweet,
a blood-red rose that titillates my nose,
a red so red, it radiates with heat.
I fear my wanting you,
and feeling wrong for you,
but our minds roam like mariners
around the world.
We contemplate our trips,
you blowing words
across my cheek.

Dear perfect yellow leaf,
spearmint soap slips
along my slope of arm.
A bubble forms. I stretch,
it stays and grows,
a rainbow-flecked thin skin of haze
that glistens, pops, goodbye.
I close my eyes and find I am alone
without my bubble.
This feels like
yet another kind of trouble.
We sit on benches near a brook.
You see the clouds on cue,
the drama passing east to west.
I'm scared of my own life,
my death was very close,
my slow return took centuries.
Unsure of what to do,
lying on a bed of grass,
unsure of being yellow in July,
a perfect yellow leaf considers fate.

Dear late green leaf,
already summer thinks of fall,
forgets the spring, the rush to green.
I am the leaf, the late green leaf,
the leaf that used to safely hang
among the other leaves.
I walk away.
It's long past due.
I won't be waiting, or hoping, or happy hearing,
or best wishing you.
I will no longer care how you are coping.
Forgotten touch, save me,
if you could just.
Never mind, I'll catch some other wave.
Unless you think another way,
a certain way,
oblivion without the decadence.
I might feel lost,
peruse the word and feel bereft,
perpetually homeless,
tied to it, the longing and the loss.

Dear troubled years,
I lie awake and gaze at dark.
The fan, a steady hum.
The moon.
Feeling fills the room and longs for you.
I'll send an envelope to you. Inside,
I'll put my house, my heart, poetic tears,
the crooked pages of my rainbow pride,
and fifty troubled years.
Then the night words scatter.
Then lost in work,
the words stay hidden.
As if to change the world,
my words could matter.
Syntax cut from cosmic lust.
I bang the keys.
I dance on air but never fly.
My drawings disappear inside a breeze.
Then pen and paper,
with words, I am,
and solitude becomes my diadem.

Dear end of time,
I drive lorn hills alone.
The miners are alive, then dead.
This is my work, my home,
my lover. You say that's fine,
your body's busy elsewhere
till the end of time.
My love, I cannot find the form
to name my sighs.
My theory dies.
My love, give me faith that I can rise
and say that this is such and such or so and so,
and yes,
that is correct, and this I know.
I feel your fingers touch my face,
but you're not there.
I feel the form will let me rest
forever in your arms.
I hope to hold and kiss you in the dark,
and so I turn
to burning words.

Elegy for Charlotte Mew

My heart drifts down, red-brown, a falling fall leaf.
Release, release, not knowing ground, a small leaf.

I dream you are beside me on a couch,
your blouse is white, I tremble, you are all leaf.

Do I not move the sun rootbound in summer
and fill your queenly crown with standing tall leaf?

Green of delight debarked despairing, lost.
Poem and letter flaming downfall, leaf.

Remember I gave you rings and poise and shimmer?
Who gave you shade is now a shadow thrall leaf.

My words were crimes were loves were leaves were smoke
Were gay were bashed were kiss were masked ball leaf.

You knew the seamstress never could repair us.
You knew November is my dance hall leaf.

With merriment no more, decay, embrace me,
at one with sky and dirt, a stone wall leaf.

Singular Heart

My heart hurts so. It slides like eels
in an aquarium.
Sucking its little cage, it feels
the slop of meriam

weighty and wildebeest, the squeeze
of skeleton and time.
It hums, a hive of bumblebees,
my honey, my sublime.

It aches for you. It is the road
you rambled on. It pines
and croaks and taps a secret code
for you, these very lines.

Epic

My love, when all my battles finally end
and down the cobbled hill I drive my car,
bumping on tired tires round the bend,
my body all one wound, my skin a scar;
and when bedraggled, I observe the star
rising like water to my thirsty eyes,
deep in the trembling darkness, still so far,
you wrap your arms around my world of sighs
and all my fallen angels fill the skies.

Most people have a family. I have flowers
but only in my mind. I have a view
of dying ash and oak, and sometimes showers
of snow or rain. The weather passes through
like everyone who comes and goes, but you.
You are the window of my best new year,
my faithful point of view, my lovely coo,
my apple crunch, my fresh warm bread, my cheer,
and in my wild poetic dreams, my dear.

I wake up empty, emptier than ever,
and naked cuddled close to my abyss
who strokes my nape and whispers *never, never,*
will I accept the ruins of your kiss.
Put on my crumbling clothes and reminisce
about the nothing day and nothing night
and say, it will be good, it will be bliss,
the soup is on the stove with all its might,
and though I have no language, I can write.

Cannot control the thunder

Are there no dancers on this solemn square?
Come come, she breathes, come violin my dreams.

Her penetrating Bach cantata beats
its blacksweet wings within my dreams.

Hallucinate her name her name her name
Mmm open open oh! Light! Pin my dreams!

Away nightmares! Unspook and spin my dreams.
You, you, my soothing pet, begin my dreams.

Hieroglyphics

Thunder's font is beautiful, dovelike, Sappho.
Thunder sings and clings to me, silence tells me
you are mist or water, and rain is scrawling
  runes on the water

where you are, so distant, your face in showers.
Jade, tornado green, then a slate gray changing
dull and gray, then fire and silver sparkles,
  silence, where are you?

waves reflect you, water is leaping higher,
tree by tree. They lean towards you, weaker branches
scorched by lightning, burnt by a gust of gorgeous
  thundering swallows.

You pierce me

You pierce me with a thousand styles of kindness.
Your lightning shocks the earth with miles of kindness.

While I'm asleep all night in my soft bed,
you pave my bedroom floor with tiles of kindness.

Like some mad queen insatiable for gold,
I hoard and count your priceless piles of kindness.

How could I help but loosen all my armor?
How could I not succumb to wiles of kindness?

The letter never sent, the gaze not met,
the words unsaid—all safe in files of kindness.

My terror at the thought of losing you,
as if I had you, oh! the trials of kindness.

What current took me out to sea, and now
turns me towards your murmuring isles of kindness?

You flood the sky of my unmarried dark,
you rise, a little moon with smiles of kindness.

The Acrobats

I spend my solo life in windy spaces,
way up above the throng, no safety net
below, exposed to row on row of faces
fixed on the acrobats in silhouette.
I'll fall with one misstep or if the wire
splits or my fingers slip. I climb the rungs,
trembling, trembling. Rising higher, higher,
I cough out all the fumbles in my lungs,
and here's my tiny platform, just a disk
that fits my feet. From here, I leap and swing
into the flashing lights, familiar with the risk
by now, but shocked to see you stand and fling
yourself from your own platform over there
and catch me from your swing through the thin air.

Muse of O

O lover, O my sweet sweet sweet sweet lover,
the O-ing letters of our alphabet
hide in the trees where wild blue tit birds hover
and make ah-sighs, their hearty beaks dew-wet,
their yellow-feather sides astir with fret.
You letter me, I letter you, we go
so high above the trees to do the pet
and bee, then with our O, we go below.
Down here, a hurricane begins to blow
and blow the leaves like Braille without a finger.
We tattoo dictionaries so we know
the tongue we speak, and let our language linger.
This is a sweet sweet sweet sweet afternoon,
the education of our lover rune.

Notes

"The Stone Insanity" - The title is from "Letter to the Front" by Muriel Rukeyser.

"The Only Home I Know" won honorable mention in the New England Shakespeare Festival Sonnet Contest.

"Sea de Sade" - "unmoored from the mother ship of culture" is a quote from Camille Paglia.

"Obodowka Cemetery" - One of the few facts I know about my mother is that her maiden name is Kittner. With the help of a few German speakers, I translated this poem by Shoah poet, Alfred Kittner (1906-1991). Many thanks to Seree Cohen Zohar, Martin Rocek, Andrés Nader, Adam Elgar, and Roberta Saltzman.

"Arondeus" - Willem Arondeus (1894-1943) is a hero of the Dutch Resistance and saved the lives of many Dutch citizens.

"The Ozarks in 2004" is dedicated to Holly Baggett.

"The Acrobats" won honorable mention in the Helen Schaible International Sonnet Contest.

Acknowledgments

My thanks to the editors of the following publications, in which these poems first appeared:

American Arts Quarterly: "Three Crowns of Misfortune"

American Journal of Nursing: "Madhouse"

Blue Lyra Review: "Singular Heart"

Bridges: A Jewish Feminist Journal: "I Learn Today My Mother Lied"

Chronicles: "The Acrobats"

Enchanted Conversation: "How Beautiful She Is," "The Prince of Glass," and "Night of Snow"

Eyewear: "Somewhere Along the Spectrum"

Light Quarterly: "Why won't you love me?"

Literary Imagination: "Witness This"

Measure: "Midnight Kitchen"

Mezzo Cammin: "A Tragedy of Flowers," "Garden State After the War," "Dinner," and "Wolf"

OCHO: "Sea de Sade" and "Orphic Chant"

Poetry Northeast: "Plaintive Note Motel," "The Mother's Buttons," and "Beginning with a Line from *Paradise Lost*"

Snakeskin: "Charlotte Mew"

The Lyric: "Cuckoo Father"

The Raintown Review: "You pierce me"

The Rotary Dial: "Done"

Writers Among Artists: "Baptist Faggot Dinosaur"

Thanks also to the editors who reprinted these poems:

Lady Business (Sibling Rivalry Press, 2012): "Orphic Chant" and "Baptist Faggot Dinosaur"

Lilt: "Witness This"

Obsession: Sestinas in the 21st Century (University Press of New England, 2014): "A Tragedy of Flowers"

Sixty-Six: The Journal of Sonnet Studies: "Sea de Sade" and "Cuckoo Father"

Street Spirit: "Why won't you love me?"

Headmistress Press Books

Seed - Janice Gould
The Princess of Pain - Carolyn Gage & Sudie Rakusin
She/Her/Hers - Amy Lauren
Spoiled Meat - Nicole Santalucia
Cake - Jen Rouse
The Salt and the Song - Virginia Petrucci
mad girl's crush tweet - summer jade leavitt
Saturn coming out of its Retrograde - Briana Roldan
i am this girl - gina marie bernard
Week/End - Sarah Duncan
My Girl's Green Jacket - Mary Meriam
Nuts in Nutland - Mary Meriam, Hannah Barrett
Lovely - Lesléa Newman
Teeth & Teeth - Robin Reagler
How Distant the City - Freesia McKee
Shopgirls - Marissa Higgins
Riddle - Diane Fortney
When She Woke She Was an Open Field - Hilary Brown
God With Us - Amy Lauren
A Crown of Violets - Renée Vivien tr. Samantha Pious
Fireworks in the Graveyard - Joy Ladin
Social Dance - Carolyn Boll
The Force of Gratitude - Janice Gould
Spine - Sarah Caulfield
Diatribe from the Library - Farrell Greenwald Brenner
Blind Girl Grunt - Constance Merritt
Acid and Tender - Jen Rouse
Beautiful Machinery - Wendy DeGroat
Odd Mercy - Gail Thomas

The Great Scissor Hunt - Jessica K. Hylton
A Bracelet of Honeybees - Lynn Strongin
Whirlwind @ Lesbos - Risa Denenberg
The Body's Alphabet - Ann Tweedy
First name Barbie last name Doll - Maureen Bocka
Heaven to Me - Abe Louise Young
Sticky - Carter Steinmann
Tiger Laughs When You Push - Ruth Lehrer
Night Ringing - Laura Foley
Paper Cranes - Dinah Dietrich
On Loving a Saudi Girl - Carina Yun
The Burn Poems - Lynn Strongin
I Carry My Mother - Lesléa Newman
Distant Music - Joan Annsfire
The Awful Suicidal Swans - Flower Conroy
Joy Street - Laura Foley
Chiaroscuro Kisses - G.L. Morrison
The Lillian Trilogy - Mary Meriam
Lady of the Moon - Amy Lowell, Lillian Faderman, Mary Meriam
Irresistible Sonnets - ed. Mary Meriam
Lavender Review - ed. Mary Meriam

www.ingramcontent.com/pod-product-compliance
Lightning Source LLC
LaVergne TN
LVHW030922080826
845145LV00013B/3016

* 9 7 8 0 6 1 5 8 3 0 5 6 8 *